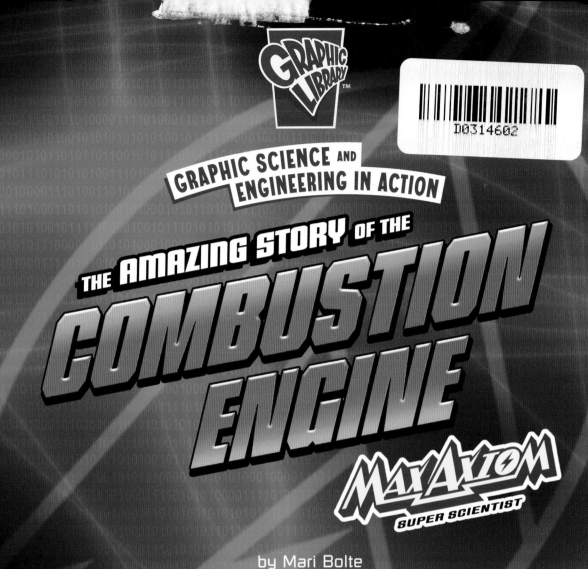

GRAPHIC LIBRARY ™

GRAPHIC SCIENCE AND ENGINEERING IN ACTION

THE AMAZING STORY OF THE COMBUSTION ENGINE

MAX AXIOM SUPER SCIENTIST

by Mari Bolte

illustrated by Pop Art Properties

Aberdeenshire

3139192

Raintree is an imprint of Capstone Global Library Limited,
a company incorporated in England and Wales having its registered office at
7 Pilgrim Street, London, EC4V 6LB – Registered company number: 6695582

www.raintreepublishers.co.uk
myorders@raintreepublishers.co.uk

Text © Capstone Global Library Limited 2014
First published in paperback in 2014
The moral rights of the proprietor have been asserted.

All rights reserved. No part of this publication may be reproduced in any form or by
any means (including photocopying or storing it in any medium by electronic means
and whether or not transiently or incidentally to some other use of this publication)
without the written permission of the copyright owner, except in accordance with the
provisions of the Copyright, Designs and Patents Act 1988 or under the terms of a
licence issued by the Copyright Licensing Agency, Saffron House, 6–10 Kirby Street,
London EC1N 8TS (www.cla.co.uk). Applications for the copyright owner's written
permission should be addressed to the publisher.

Edited by Christopher L. Harbo and James Benefield
Designed by Ted Williams
Cover art by Marcelo Baez
Originated by Capstone Global Library Ltd
Production by Helen McCreath
Media research by Wanda Winch
Printed and bound in China

Photo Credits: Shutterstock: PHB.cz(Richard Semik), 7, sima, 19

ISBN 978 1 4062 7972 6
18 17 16 15 14
10 9 8 7 6 5 4 3 2 1

British Library Cataloguing in Publication Data
A full catalogue record for this book is available from the British Library.

We would like to thank Margaret Wooldridge, of the University of Michigan (Ann
Arbor), for her invaluable help in the preparation of this book.

All the internet addresses (URLs) given in this book were valid at the time
of going to press. However, due to the dynamic nature of the internet, some addresses
may have changed, or sites may have changed or ceased to exist since publication.
While the author and publisher regret any inconvenience this may cause
readers, no responsibility for any such changes can be accepted
by either the author or the publisher.

TABLE of CONTENTS

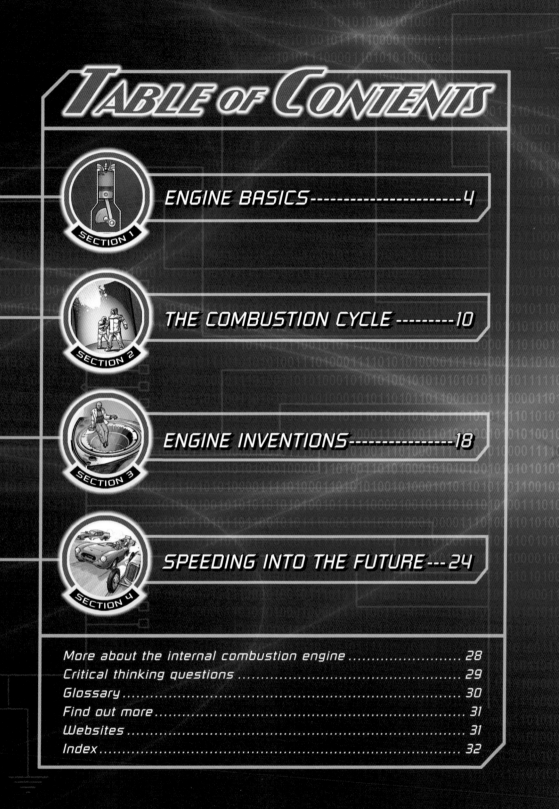

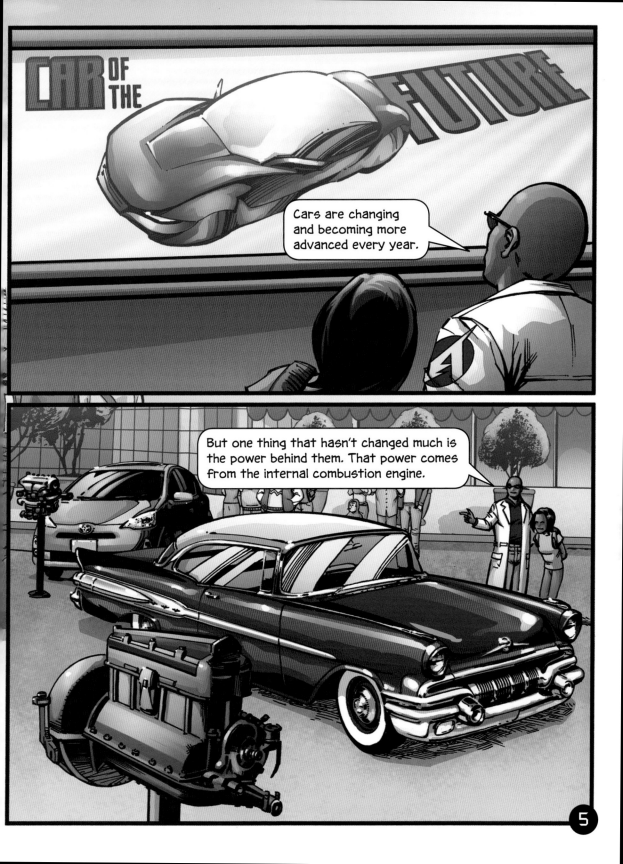

When combustion takes place in the small space of an engine, a lot of energy is released.

VVROOM!! VVROOM!!

An engine repeats the combustion process hundreds of times a minute.

Cars use the energy created by combustion to move.

EXTERNAL COMBUSTION ENGINES

Fuel burns inside the engine during internal combustion. External combustion takes place outside the engine. For example, steam engines are a form of external combustion. Fuel burns outside the engine and is used to create steam. The steam powers the engine. External combustion engines can use fuels such as wood, coal and oil.

Before learning how combustion works, we need to look at the parts that help the car run.

Inside each cylinder is a piston. The piston moves up and down in the cylinder.

The up-and-down motion made by the piston is why this engine is also called a reciprocating engine.

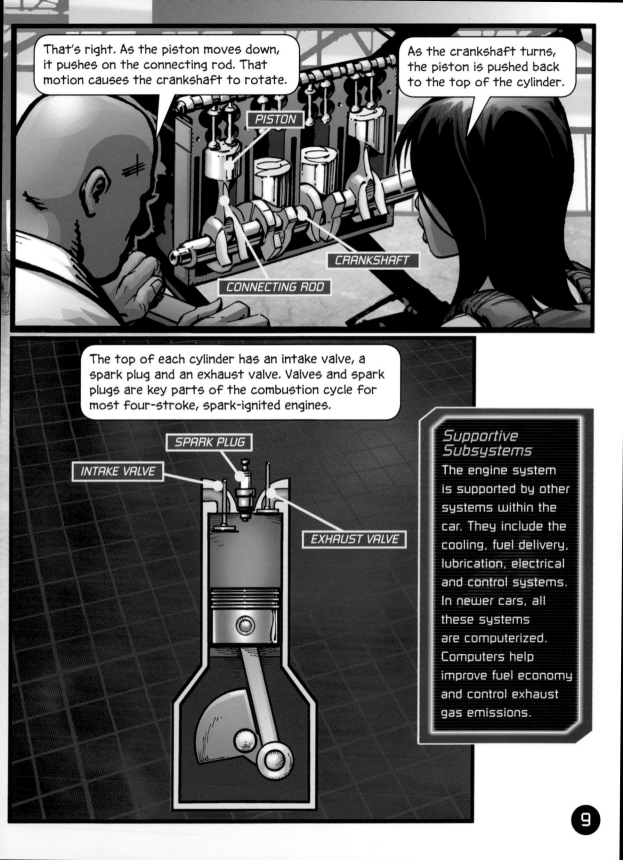

That's right. As the piston moves down, it pushes on the connecting rod. That motion causes the crankshaft to rotate.

As the crankshaft turns, the piston is pushed back to the top of the cylinder.

PISTON

CRANKSHAFT

CONNECTING ROD

The top of each cylinder has an intake valve, a spark plug and an exhaust valve. Valves and spark plugs are key parts of the combustion cycle for most four-stroke, spark-ignited engines.

SPARK PLUG

INTAKE VALVE

EXHAUST VALVE

Supportive Subsystems

The engine system is supported by other systems within the car. They include the cooling, fuel delivery, lubrication, electrical and control systems. In newer cars, all these systems are computerized. Computers help improve fuel economy and control exhaust gas emissions.

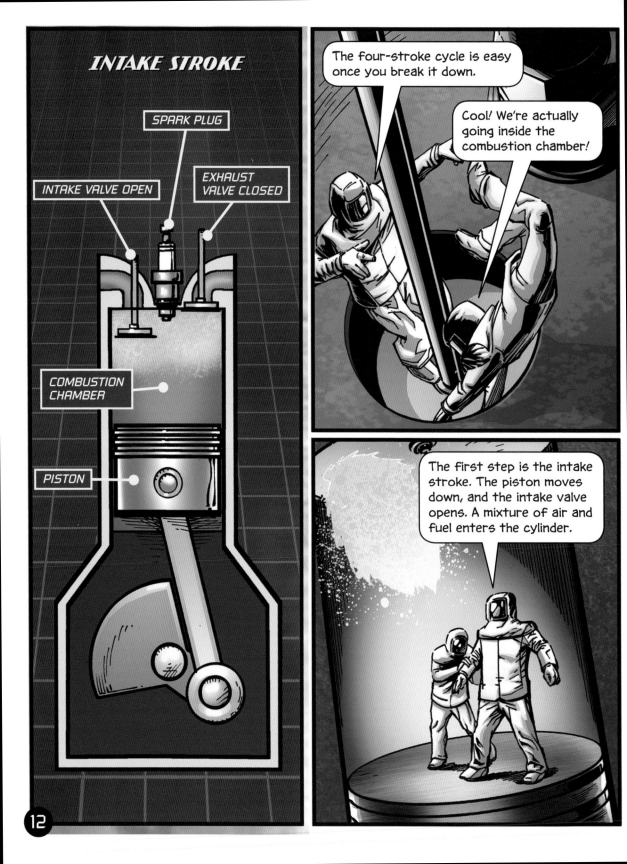

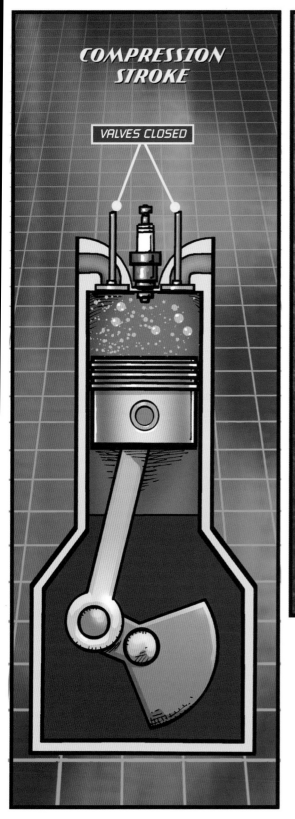

COMPRESSION STROKE

VALVES CLOSED

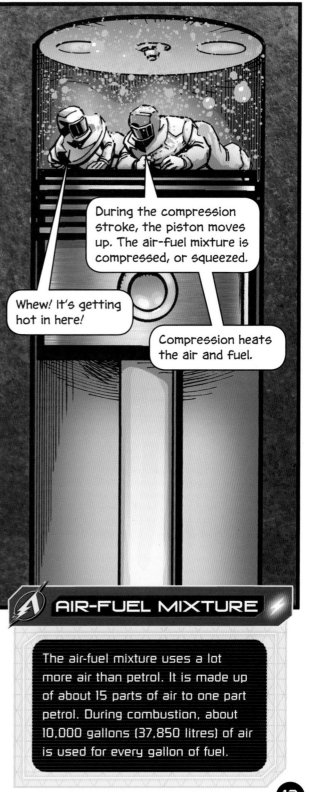

During the compression stroke, the piston moves up. The air-fuel mixture is compressed, or squeezed.

Whew! It's getting hot in here!

Compression heats the air and fuel.

AIR-FUEL MIXTURE

The air-fuel mixture uses a lot more air than petrol. It is made up of about 15 parts of air to one part petrol. During combustion, about 10,000 gallons (37,850 litres) of air is used for every gallon of fuel.

COMBUSTION STROKE

VALVES CLOSED

SPARK PLUG FIRING

When the piston reaches the top of the stroke, the spark plug fires. The heated air-fuel mixture allows the spark to create flames.

These flames race across the cylinder and the hot gases expand rapidly.

The rapidly expanding gases drive the piston to the bottom of the combustion chamber.

WHEEE!!!

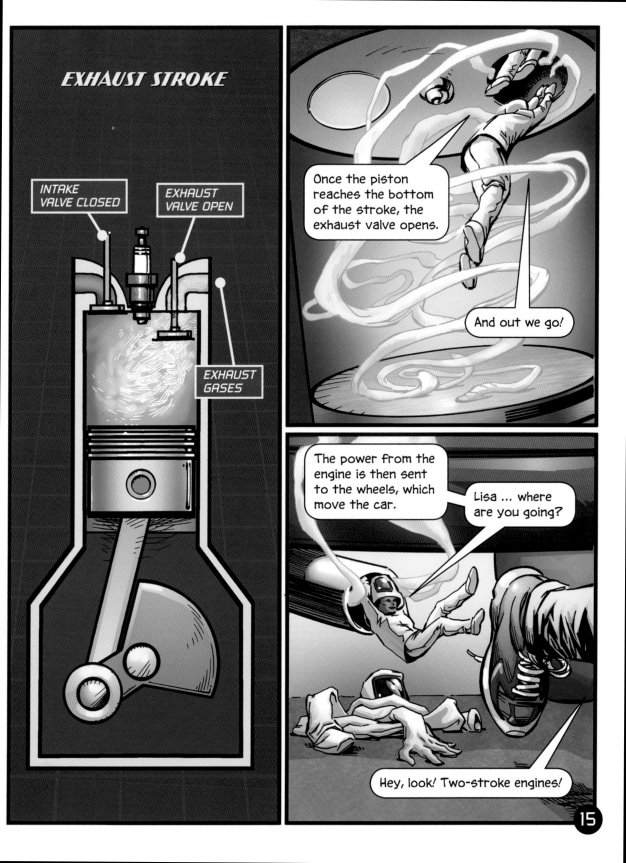

It sounds like a room full of chainsaws!

That'd be the two-stroke engine at work.

What's the difference between two-stroke and four-stroke engines?

Two-stroke engines have only compression and combustion strokes. Intake and exhaust strokes happen too, but they aren't their own steps.

The air-fuel mixture is also mixed with oil, for lubrication.

The two-stroke engine uses the space above and below the piston. The transfer port pushes the air-fuel mixture from the lower part of the cylinder to the upper part.

The fresh gases force the used gases out the open exhaust port.

As the piston rises, it closes both the transfer port and the exhaust port.

Now the air-fuel mixture is compressed. At the same time, fresh air-fuel is drawn into the lower part of the cylinder. The compressed mixture is sparked, driving the piston downward. Then the two-stroke cycle starts again.

TRANSFER PORT

EXHAUST PORT

DOWNSTROKE

UPSTROKE

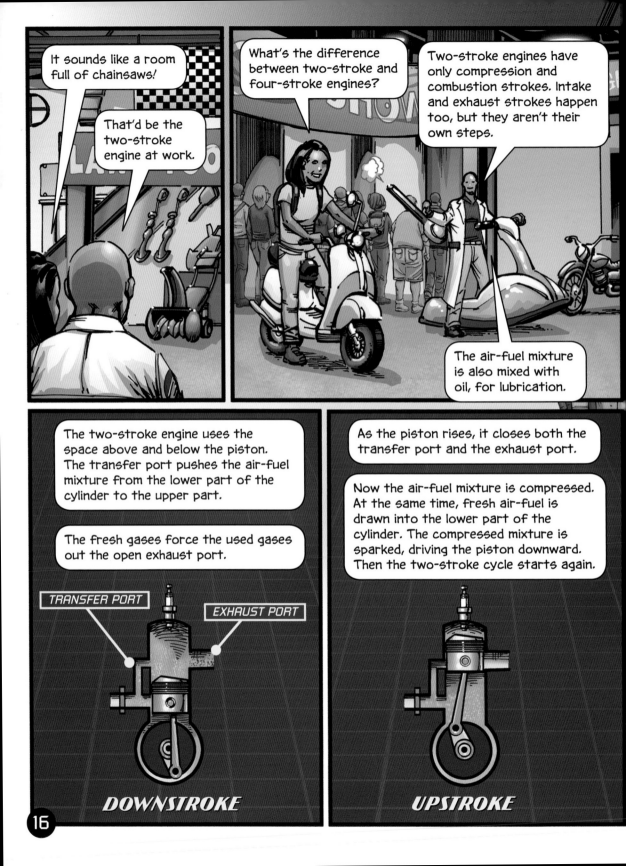

BURNING OIL

Two-stroke engines use 20 millilitres of oil per litre of petrol. If a car engine worked the same way, 3.8 litres (1 gallon) of oil would be burned every 1,600 kilometres (1,000 miles). The average driver would create a lot more pollution by burning through more than 21 litres of oil every year.

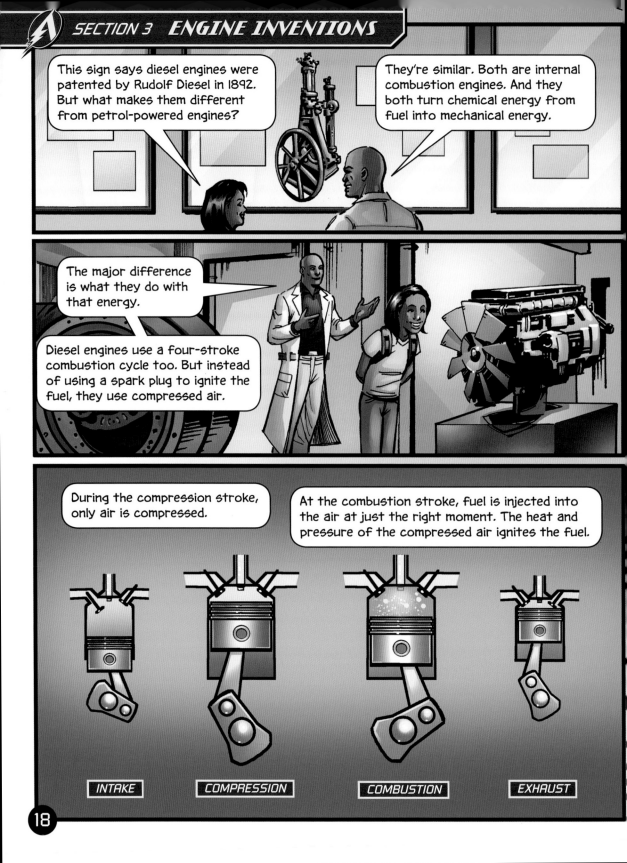

This sign says diesel engines were patented by Rudolf Diesel in 1892. But what makes them different from petrol-powered engines?

They're similar. Both are internal combustion engines. And they both turn chemical energy from fuel into mechanical energy.

The major difference is what they do with that energy.

Diesel engines use a four-stroke combustion cycle too. But instead of using a spark plug to ignite the fuel, they use compressed air.

During the compression stroke, only air is compressed.

At the combustion stroke, fuel is injected into the air at just the right moment. The heat and pressure of the compressed air ignites the fuel.

INTAKE

COMPRESSION

COMBUSTION

EXHAUST

Cars that run on diesel get better mileage than unleaded petrol engines. Diesel engines also provide a lot of power at low speeds.

That's why heavy movers like farm equipment, freight trucks, ships and locomotives use diesel.

GAS

But diesel releases more nitrogen oxides and soot than regular petrol engines. These emissions lead to acid rain, smog and breathing problems for some people.

BIODIESEL

ACCESS GRANTED: MAX AXIOM

Biodiesel is an alternative fuel made from plant oils or animal fats. It usually produces less soot than diesel made from fossil fuels. It's also biodegradable. Biodiesel made from plant matter also helps reduce greenhouse gases released by engines. Biodiesel can be used by itself or blended with regular diesel.

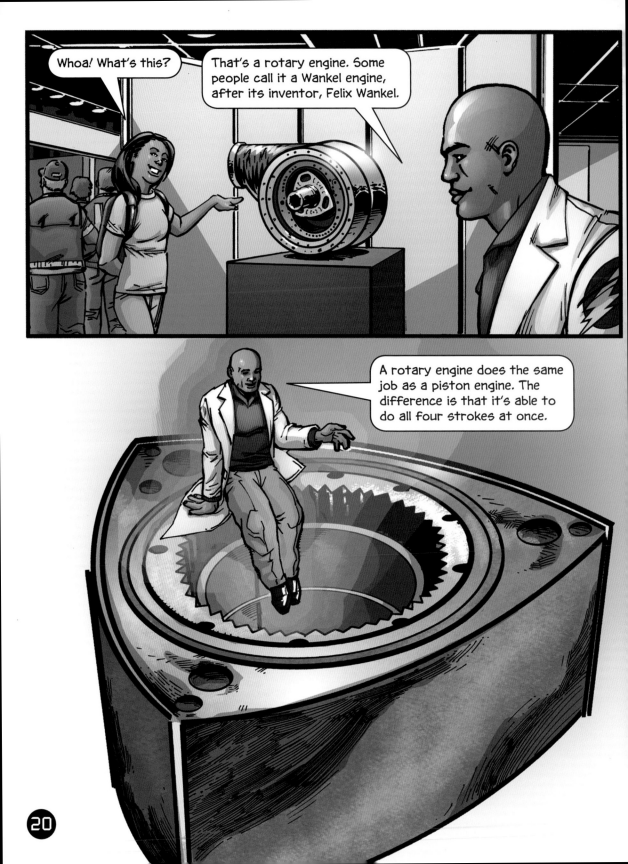

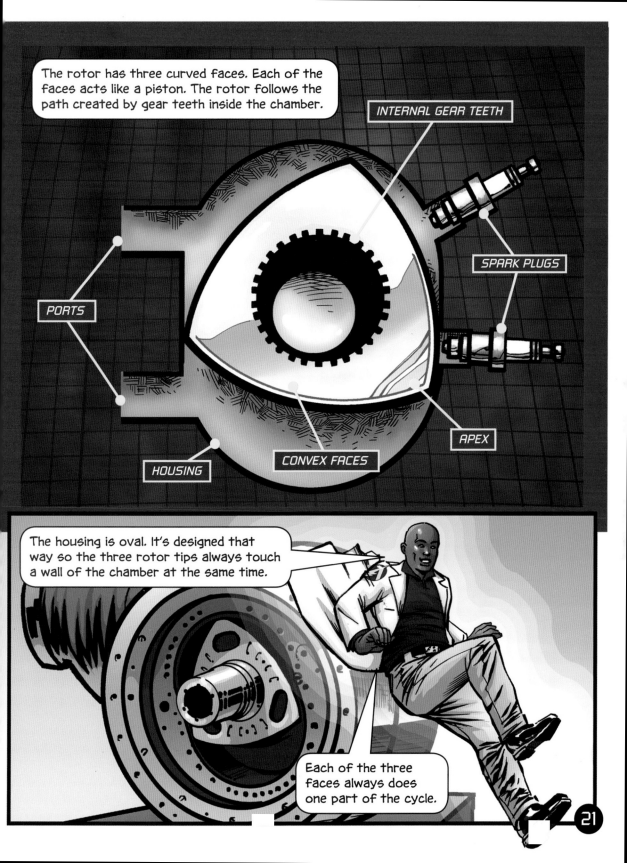

The rotor has three curved faces. Each of the faces acts like a piston. The rotor follows the path created by gear teeth inside the chamber.

INTERNAL GEAR TEETH

SPARK PLUGS

PORTS

APEX

CONVEX FACES

HOUSING

The housing is oval. It's designed that way so the three rotor tips always touch a wall of the chamber at the same time.

Each of the three faces always does one part of the cycle.

Before the intake stroke, the volume of that chamber is at its smallest. As the rotor moves past the intake port, the chamber expands, drawing air-fuel in. When the peak of the rotor moves past the port, the chamber is sealed.

INTAKE

As the rotor continues its motion, the chamber gets smaller. This motion compresses the air-fuel mixture. By the time the rotor reaches the spark plugs, the chamber is again at its smallest.

COMPRESSION

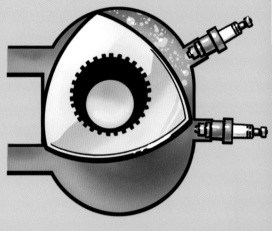

Rotary engines have two spark plugs. These plugs ensure the flame spreads quickly. The air-fuel mixture ignites, keeping the rotor moving.

COMBUSTION

SPARK PLUG

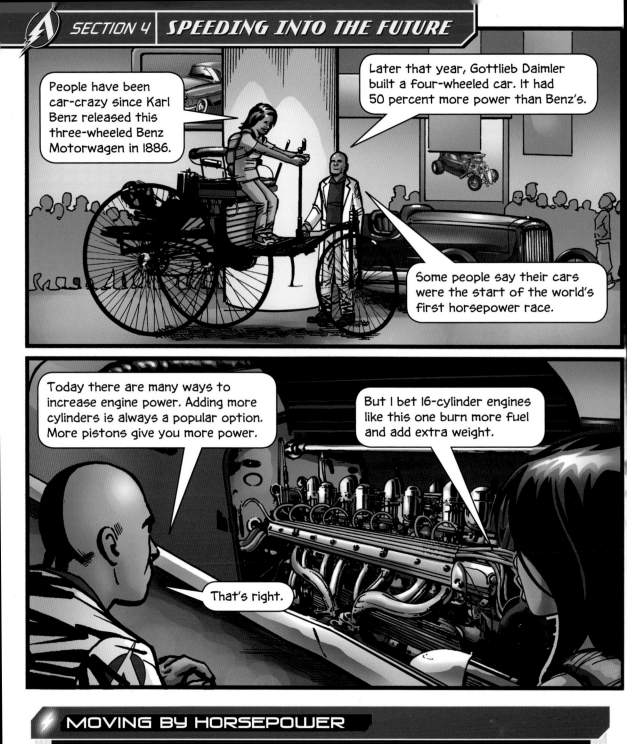

People have been car-crazy since Karl Benz released this three-wheeled Benz Motorwagen in 1886.

Later that year, Gottlieb Daimler built a four-wheeled car. It had 50 percent more power than Benz's.

Some people say their cars were the start of the world's first horsepower race.

Today there are many ways to increase engine power. Adding more cylinders is always a popular option. More pistons give you more power.

But I bet 16-cylinder engines like this one burn more fuel and add extra weight.

That's right.

MOVING BY HORSEPOWER

Horsepower is the measurement of an engine's ability to do work. One horsepower equals the amount of work it would take to lift 250 kilograms (550 pounds), 31 centimetres (1 foot) in one second.

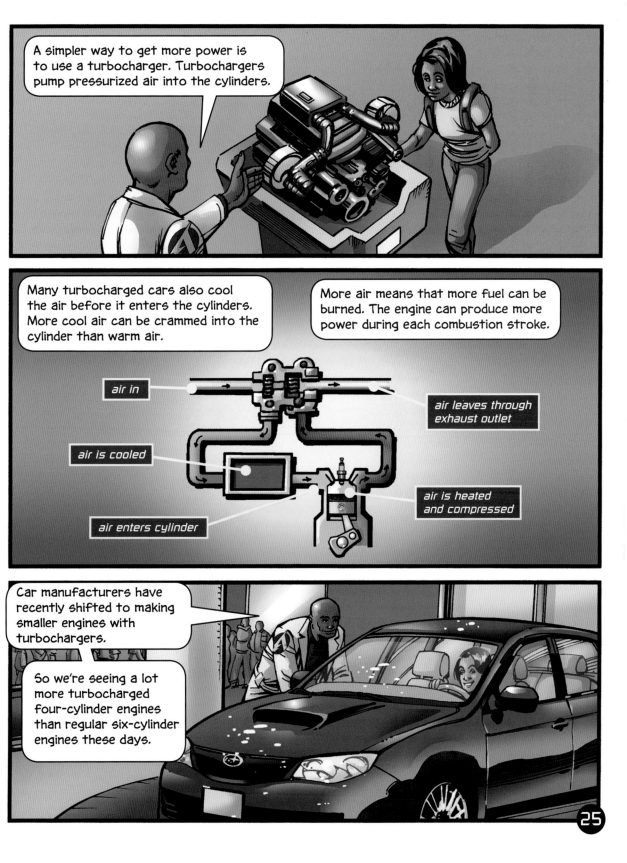

A simpler way to get more power is to use a turbocharger. Turbochargers pump pressurized air into the cylinders.

Many turbocharged cars also cool the air before it enters the cylinders. More cool air can be crammed into the cylinder than warm air.

More air means that more fuel can be burned. The engine can produce more power during each combustion stroke.

air in

air leaves through exhaust outlet

air is cooled

air is heated and compressed

air enters cylinder

Car manufacturers have recently shifted to making smaller engines with turbochargers.

So we're seeing a lot more turbocharged four-cylinder engines than regular six-cylinder engines these days.

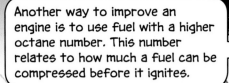

Another way to improve an engine is to use fuel with a higher octane number. This number relates to how much a fuel can be compressed before it ignites.

The higher the number, the more compression the fuel can take.

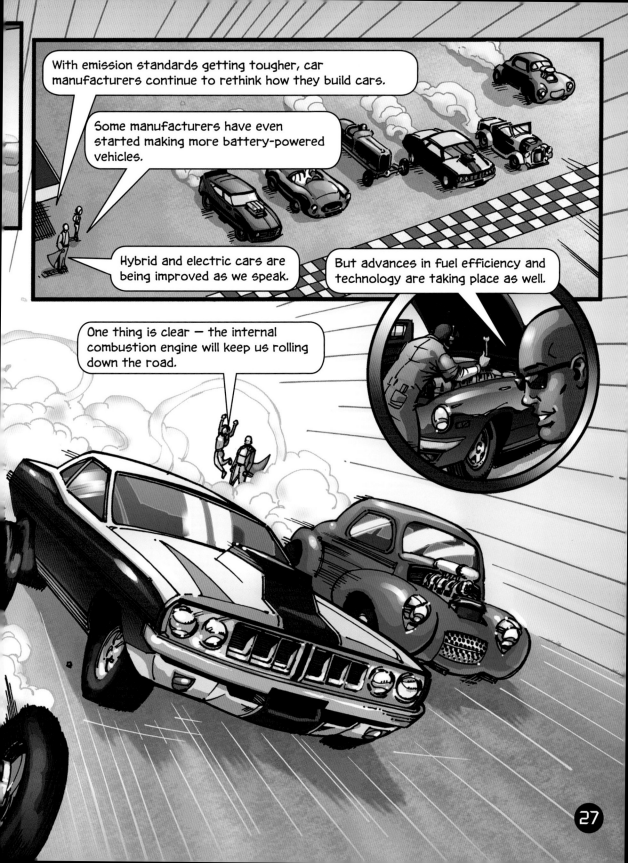

MORE ABOUT THE
INTERNAL COMBUSTION ENGINE

The first general-use internal combustion engine was built by Étienne Lenoir in 1860. It was a two-stroke engine that used a mixture of coal gas and air.

Most car engines add fuel into the cylinder during the intake stroke. Then the fuel is compressed. Normally only the spark should ignite the air-fuel mixture. But if the air is compressed too much, the mixture ignites spontaneously. This explosion causes a loud noise known as knocking. Knocking creates extra heat and can damage the engine.

Unleaded petrol and diesel are called fossil fuels. They are made from oil formed by plants and animals that lived millions of years ago. Biofuels and biodiesel are made from plants and animals living today. In 2012 the United States produced more than 3.6 billion litres (960 million gallons) of biodiesel.

Petrol gives you a lot of energy for a small amount of fuel. An average car can travel 644 km (400 miles) on a single tank of petrol. An electric car would have to be recharged at least once over the same distance. A hydrogen car would need a huge fuel tank or be able to compress the hydrogen to very high pressures. Even biofuel wouldn't get you quite as far as petrol if you used the same volume fuel tank.

Hybrid cars use power from both an engine and an electric motor. The motor takes some of the demand off the engine, which means less petrol is used. However, hybrids require complex and expensive technology to control the engine and motor together.

CRITICAL THINKING QUESTIONS

1. On pages 10 and 11, the author shows Max and Lisa travelling back to the past. Why do you think the author wrote the scene this way? How does it help your understanding of the internal combustion engine?

2. On page 17, a man uses a chainsaw as Max and Lisa explain two-stroke engines. Make a list of other tools or vehicles you think might use two-stroke engines. Why would these items benefit from a two-stroke instead of a four-stroke engine?

3. Why is air such an important part of the combustion cycle? Explain how turbochargers use air and why they give engines more power.

MORE ABOUT

Real name: Maxwell J. Axiom
Hometown: Seattle, USA
Height: 1.85m Weight: 87kg
Eyes: Brown   Hair: None

Super capabilities: Super intelligence; able to shrink to the size of an atom; sunglasses give x-ray vision; lab coat allows for travel through time and space.

Origin: Since birth, Max Axiom seemed destined for greatness. His mother, a marine biologist, taught her son about the mysteries of the sea. His father, a nuclear physicist and volunteer park ranger, schooled Max on the wonders of earth and sky.

One day on a wilderness hike, a megacharged lightning bolt struck Max with blinding fury. When he awoke, Max discovered a newfound energy and set out to learn as much about science as possible. He travelled the globe earning degrees in every aspect of the field. Upon his return, he was ready to share his knowledge and new identity with the world. He had become Max Axiom, Super Scientist.

combustion (kuhm-BUS-chuhn) – the process of burning a fuel with air

compression (kuhm-PRESH-uhn) – the reduction of the volume of a system by applying a force

cylinder (SI-luhn-duhr) – a hollow area inside an engine in which fuel burns to create power

emissions (ee-MI-shuhnz) – gases and particles released into the air by an engine

exhaust (eg-ZORST) – the waste gases produced by an engine

horsepower (HORSS-pow-ur) – a unit for measuring the power of an engine

hybrid (HYE-brid) – a mix of two different types of technologies; hybrid engines run on electricity and petrol or diesel fuel

ignite (ig-NITE) – to start combustion

lubrication (loo-bruh-KAY-shuhn) – the addition of a substance, such as oil, to reduce friction and heat generated by parts rubbing against each other

octane number (OK-tang NUM-bur) – a measure of how much a fuel can be compressed before it ignites

piston (PIS-tuhn) – part of an engine that moves up and down within a cylinder

rotor (ROE-tur) – the part of an engine or other machine that turns or rotates

valve (VALV) – a movable part that controls the flow of liquid or gas through a pipe or opening

Find Out More

Car Science, Richard Hammond, (Dorling Kindersley, 2011)

Shop Tech: The Science of Cars (Everyday Science), Karen Latchana Kenney (Compass Point Books, 2012)

Transport: Find Out About Engines, Gravity and Flight with 40 Great Experiments and Projects (Hands on Science), Chris Oxley (Southwater, 2008)

Who Invented the Automobile? (Breakthroughs in Science and Technology), Brian Williams (Arcturus Publishing, 2010)

Websites

www.grc.nasa.gov/WWW/K-12/airplane/engopt.html

On this website, you can watch an amazing animation of part of a really early aeroplane engine.

www.sciencekids.co.nz/videos/engineering/carengine.html

Watch a video of how a car engine actually works!

www.speedace.info/internal_combustion_engine.htm

Want to go into more detail about the combustion engines? This is a good place to start!